Ben Zephaniah: My Story

Written by Benjamin Zephaniah
Illustrated by Victor Ambrus

Contents

From Jamaica to England

My parents came to England in 1954. It was at a time when there were a lot of jobs – road sweeping, driving buses and stuff like that. My mum and her sister were walking down the street in Jamaica one day and they saw this poster saying, "Come to the mother country, where the streets are paved with gold, there are jobs **galore**."

My mum wanted to go, she wanted to do something with her life. She thought that Jamaica was a small island and Britain was a big place with **opportunities**.

one of the ships that brought people from the Caribbean to England in the 1940s and 1950s

She didn't want to be stuck in St Elizabeth picking potatoes all her life. So my uncle gave her the money for the fare, which was only about £20, and she got on a ship and came.

When she got here she mentioned to somebody that she'd like to do nursing, and they told her to go to Birmingham, so that's what she did.

A busy house

Hockley in the 1960s

I was born in Aston. I don't really remember that so much, but then we moved to Hockley, because we got our own council house, and I remember that. Hockley was very white – very poor, but very white. I remember that our house had no bathroom. We just had an old tin bath in the **communal** back garden.

We had a busy household, because I've got seven brothers and sisters. There's me and my twin sister, and there's another set of twins too. I'm the oldest, and because I'm the oldest, I was the boss for a long while. I remember that when the school over the road from us closed down, I went over and got all these exercise books and brought them into the house during the school holidays. I made all my brothers and sisters go to "school", with me as the teacher. They didn't want to but I made them do it – because I was the boss!

I actually really liked a busy house, a house with lots of kids and lots of noise. Somebody was always crying, somebody was always cut, somebody was always hurt, and there was no such thing as privacy!

We had a double bed, and there'd be two up and two down, though we all swapped around so you were never sharing with the same person. I worked out who I wanted to share with by seeing whose feet were the least smelly!

We were really poor, and didn't get new things very often. There was only one comb in the house, and sometimes it would go missing and Mum would have to comb everybody's hair with a fork!

As our shoes wore out, instead of buying a new pair, our dad would make new soles out of cardboard, so that they lasted longer. He'd cut out the shape of the shoe in the cardboard, and stick it to the bottom of the shoe. It was all right if it was dry, but if it was wet it was horrible. I remember one day watching my brother walking and as he walked you could just see a bit of the cardboard. So I got him to watch me, and when he said he could see the cardboard on my shoes too, it completely changed the way I walked. I stopped lifting my foot up behind me, because I didn't want the other kids to see the cardboard.

School days

I remember my first day at school. Me and my sister were the only black children there and we were in the same class so I said to her, "You've got to be tough, don't let anybody put you down." But she still got really upset and cried a lot.

I was trying to be the tough guy, and my sister just cried, she cried all day and you could hear her anywhere they put her in the school. It was quite embarrassing so I decided to distance myself from her a bit, so people didn't think we were the same. So she was crying and there I was, her twin brother, trying to **disassociate** myself from her.

But I did stand up for my brothers and sisters. When they all joined the school it was my job to look after them. If there was ever a problem in the playground I didn't fight, I'd just look out for them and we'd hang out in a big gang.

It was a very old-fashioned school, very strict. I'd call it Victorian: old fashioned teachers – hair in buns, really bossy. Just after me and my sister arrived, as a kind of celebration they encouraged all the kids to bring in a **golliwog** to "impress young Benjamin". It wasn't really seen as racist at the time but I didn't really like it much there.

Food, glorious food

One good thing about school was the dinner. We got free
school meals and they were treats for us because the food we
had at home was very Jamaican, so this was our chance to
have English food: pies, mashed potato and mushy peas!
I was a very **reluctant** meat eater though, I never really
liked meat. I preferred vegetables, fruit and things like cake
and custard, so sometimes I'd skip the dinner part and just
have pudding, pudding, pudding, pudding!

Run, run, run

I was very sporty at school.
I loved football, and running –
sprinting; put a jumper down
there, put a jumper down
there and I'll race you.
I was really good at sprinting.
That meant I was really good
at kiss chase, which was my
favourite sport of all!

Even in football I didn't like the dirty tackling, but if you put me on the right wing and got the ball to me, I'd run with it. I remember playing rugby which I didn't really like, but once I got the ball I could run! My **motivation** was different: it wasn't to score a try – I just didn't want anyone tackling me!

I went to one school, for a short time, called Ward End Hall and they had this really amazing, strange sport called basketball, which wasn't played much in Britain then, and I loved that too. I was really good at it.

I didn't just like typical boys' sports though. I loved skipping, too. I was happy to skip with the girls and I loved the nursery rhymes that went with the skipping, probably because I loved poetry so much. When I was a kid I was doing little verses all the time. I loved word play, so when girls were skipping and chanting, I thought it was great fun.

One day I was sitting in assembly and the teacher said, "Boys and girls, I have some good news. We're going to have a cricket team and we have a captain for our cricket team, young Benjamin here." But cricket was a sport I didn't like, or understand. I remember the teacher said to me, "You're a born cricketer," and I thought, "I'm definitely not a born cricketer."

But they forced me to play and I broke my finger, which made me hate it even more. So I put my foot down and explained that I didn't want to be captain – or even in the team – and so they let me quit.

Trouble at home

When I was about nine years old my mum and dad split up.
I went with my mum, and my brothers and sisters stayed
with Dad.

We had to move around a lot because Dad kept finding us and
he could be quite violent. Sometimes we'd find a little bedsit,
and we'd be there for a week or so and then we'd have to
move on because Dad found out where we were.

Sometimes we'd have to change our names so he couldn't find us. We never slept on the street, but we had to knock on doors sometimes and ask to be put up. I was never lonely or sad because I made friends and had a good time wherever I was. I'd go into the street and see if the local kids would play football with me. That's just what you did. As bad as things were, the most important thing for me, for my life, was having fun, so once my mum had told me the rules of the house I'd go and find some friends to play with, and that was it.

Every time we moved I went to a different school. Once, I was only at the school for a day – it was a boys' school and I hated it – but most of the time I'd stay for a couple of weeks or a couple of months. Every time Mum moved, she'd find me a local school, so I've been to a lot of schools in a lot of cities.

I got used to moving around and it wasn't too bad because there weren't ever any long goodbyes: I'd come home from school and Mum would be packed and we'd just have to go. The only thing is that I don't have many school friends now, probably because of my **lifestyle** when I was growing up. Nobody from school really remembers me because I was only ever there for a short time.

Visits to Jamaica

Farmland in Jamaica: you can see
how much it looks like England.

It was around this time I started going to Jamaica. I first went
when I was about 12 years old. I never lived there, just
visited relatives. The place where my family comes from in
Jamaica is called St Elizabeth, and it looks just like England,
like Lincolnshire! Real countryside, farming territory.

The first thing I noticed is that time slows down there, the days
just seem longer. There's no rushing around, everybody walks
slower, it's a lot gentler and people are a lot calmer. Whenever I
used to go, people would say they could tell I wasn't from there
because of the way I walked – too fast!

The way families are in Jamaica is different too – they're a lot tighter, they all sleep in the same bed, with the goat underneath, and it's very loving.

The way that people cook and share food is also very different, though sometimes I think they eat too much, because everything is celebrated with food.

Doing poetry in church

I started doing poetry when I was about five years old – that's
according to my mum, and I do have memories of it. But my
first performance was at the age of ten, in church, where
I performed songs from the Bible in a kind of poetic style.
I put a rhythm in it and a little dance and it became a bit of
a show. If they wanted some entertainment in church they'd
say, "Get the boy up," and I'd get up there and do some stuff.
But I didn't really write poetry down until I was about 21.

Life in rhyme

My mother had told us little poems for as long as I
can remember. Jamaicans do that, they've got little poems,
parables and stories to illustrate things – she taught recipes to
my sisters in rhyme. So when I heard these, I started making
my own ones and my mother says that as soon as I started
using language I used it poetically. I did it in the playground:
instead of being cool, I did funny rhymes!

So that was my early poetry. It was just about everyday things.
I didn't call it poetry, I called it playing with words. When I
was eight years old, I imagined doing poetry for a living, but
by the time I was 13 I'd forgotten all about that.

Dub poetry

I left school when I was 13 years old. My mum was very relaxed about it. She just thought I wasn't doing much there and I was better off at home with her.

By the time I was 15 I was well-known as a "dub poet" in Birmingham. Dub poetry is a dubbed version of a track, like a remix. So a poet like me speaks over an original track. Then, when you take away the music, it still sounds musical. Dub poets usually speak about important issues – politics, people's rights, and things like that.

When I was about 20, I went back to the idea I'd had when I was eight to be a poet and earn a living from it, so I moved to London to change my life.

London in the 1970s

24

I was really lucky because I met people who were performers and I'd go to concerts and stand at the side of the stage, waiting for the bands to change over so that I could cheekily ask the manager if I could go on and do a poem. They all thought I was crazy, but I did it anyway and the crowd were always really impressed and wanted more, and that's how it started. Everybody heard about the guy who'd just go on stage and hold the crowd for a good ten minutes, so bands started asking me to support them.

Stage fright

I'm lucky because I never get
stage fright. When my mum sees
me on stage, she says, "That's
my boy, that's him," because
when I'm on stage I'm at home,
I'm more at home than ever.

me with my mum

When I stand at the side of the stage I'm desperate to be on.
In fact, what's weird is that the only time I get stage fright is
if I have to make an announcement. It can be as silly as
having to ask someone to go and move their car or something,
but it throws me completely, because it's something I have
to remember. If it's just me on stage, on my own, with my
poems, then I'm happy. I've got a very bad memory, but I
never forget my poems.

on stage in Birmingham

performing at Christmas

My first book

By this point I had written quite a lot of poems, and I decided to take them to some publishers.

Some would read them, and say, "We don't have a place for this." Some would just look at me and say, "Sorry, we don't do black **Rastafarian** poetry," which is really odd because I'm a black Rastafarian, but my poetry isn't. But I kept trying, I kept trying, I kept trying, and one day I walked into a bookshop in East London, and was just what they were looking for, and that's how my first book *Pen Rhythm* was published. It's more like a booklet than a book, but it's an official book.

I remember getting my first copy, and I just looked at it, and looked at it, and looked at it and read it again and again. I'd read the proofs, but it looked different with the cover on. And then everybody started to talk about the book, they even talked about it on television and I was so proud.

This is me at one of my book signings.

Back to school

I decided to go to adult education classes, because people were calling me a writer and I was embarrassed, because I thought I couldn't write.

It was at these classes that the teacher told me I was **dyslexic**. I didn't know what it was, but then she explained and it was like a movie – all these flashbacks came from when I was at school and I'd found the work really difficult and felt really stupid, and like everyone in the class was better than me. I'd even thought that it was because reading and writing were not the kind of things that black people did – we're good at sport and singing, not reading and writing.

I'd coped by creating my own kind of code over the years, which I still use. I write **phonetically** most of the time, so I try to capture the sound of the word. For example, if I was going to write, "To be or not to be? That is the question," I'd write, "2 b or not 2 b dat is de ?" That's my code, and I just carried it on.

The important thing for me when I started writing was to capture the sound, so that when people were reading it, it was like they were hearing it. In some ways, when I started being really creative, being dyslexic was an advantage: I wasn't limited to correct English, and I still feel that freedom when I write now.

I still use my little code, and now I'm really honest with people about how long things take me. Reading scripts can be a little bit difficult, so sometimes I'll change a word in a script into my code, so that I know what it means.

The TV slot

By this time I was living in Stratford in east London, on a council estate. I asked some of my neighbours and friends if they'd read my book, and when they explained that they didn't read books I realised that there were lots of people in the country that just didn't read. And the people, a lot of people, that I really wanted to reach were those who weren't reading. So I decided to go back to performing. I wanted to take poetry into people's houses. I became more concerned with television, radio, theatre and performing on the streets again.

a council estate in east London

Channel 4 had just started, and in those days it was the station for the **minority groups**. I got a regular spot on Channel 4 just before the news to do a poem. It was a short programme, called *The Slot*, and it meant that my poems started being played on TV.

I stopped worrying about being published. I just wanted to perform. And funnily enough as soon as I'd made this decision, lots of publishers started showing an interest in my work. But it was really important to me to take poetry to people, not expect people to get poetry from bookshops.

On the road

I was performing abroad right from the beginning. In one month I actually visited every continent. I love travelling and performing in other countries. India is a favourite place of mine to perform because Indians love poetry, and the culture is so alive there. South Africa is full of poetry too. I find it embarrassing going on stage there because there are always so many better poets in the audience!

meeting my fans on a tour of India and Sri Lanka

I got really involved in black rights in South Africa during **Apartheid**, and in 1983 I recorded a song about it called "Free South Africa". It was really a tribute to **Nelson Mandela**, and I didn't know this at the time but he read my work and listened to tapes of my recordings in prison. When he was released and came to London, he asked to meet me and we sat down for about three quarters of an hour and talked. It was really weird, because he'd represented this whole struggle for justice and equality between the races, and I thanked him for all that he'd done and for not selling out, and he was going over the top thanking *me*, for my part in the struggle. But it was an amazing experience, and we're still friends, which is really important to me.

meeting Nelson Mandela

How I write

I have to feel passionate about something to write a poem on it. I want to inspire people with my poems in a way that politicians don't. I want to touch people more emotionally, so it's important to feel strongly about the subject I'm writing about.

For me, it's easier that way because if I feel strongly about something I don't have to do much research: I know why I'm writing it, and that's the best place to start.

Vegan Steven

There was a young vegan
Called Steven,
Who just would not kill for no reason,
This kid would not eat
No cheese or no meat
And he hated the foxhunting season.

For a period, in my very early 20s, when I started to get noticed, that early poetry and especially the performances were very angry, very intense. That was OK, but I realised after a while that you kind of knock people out with the politics, and actually sometimes, you can make people aware of a situation if you show them the **absurdity** of it and get them to laugh at it.

In my poem "Talking Turkeys" I gave the turkey a personality and a mum, to make people look at it differently. And I know people who were not vegetarian, but who read that poem and turned vegetarian.

I think humour is probably one of the most powerful tools, because it can keep people seated through performances and probably through reading.

I think my poems and my performances are good fun, but they make you think as well, and that's important.

Talking Turkeys!!

Be nice to yu turkeys dis christmas
Cos turkeys jus wanna hav fun
Turkeys are cool, turkeys are wicked
An every turkey has a Mum.
Be nice to yu turkeys dis christmas,
Don't eat it, keep it alive,
It could be yu mate, an not on yu plate
Say, Yo! Turkey I'm on your side.

I got lots of friends who are turkeys
An all of dem fear christmas time,
Dey wanna enjoy it, dey say humans destroyed it
An humans are out of dere mind,
Yeah, I got lots of friends who are turkeys
Dey all hav a right to a life,
Not to be caged up an genetically made up
By any farmer an his wife.

Turkeys just wanna play reggae
Turkeys just wanna hip-hop
Can yu imagine a nice young turkey saying,
"I cannot wait for de chop"?
Turkeys like getting presents,
dey wanna watch christmas TV,
Turkeys hav brains an turkeys feel pain
In many ways like yu an me.

I once knew a turkey called
Turkey
He said "Benji explain to me please,
Who put de turkey in christmas
An what happens to christmas trees?"
I said "I am not too sure turkey
But it's nothing to do wid Christ Mass
Humans get greedy an waste more dan need be
An business men mek loadsa cash".

Be nice to yu turkey dis christmas
Invite dem indoors fe sum greens
Let dem eat cake an let dem partake
In a plate of organic grown beans,
Be nice to yu turkey dis christmas
An spare dem de cut of de knife,
Join Turkeys United an dey'll be delighted
An yu will mek new friends "FOR LIFE".

visiting a school in China

I'm more playful when I write for children, but I still want to discuss the issues that are important to me. That means I have to be more creative. For example, if I wanted to write something about the space race for kids, it would be a nice little fluffy poem that also had a message. The poem has to feel soft enough, but have a sting in the tail – to make children think, like this:

Dere's a man on de moon
He's skipping an stuff,
Dere's a man on de moon
He looks very tuff,
Dere's a man on de moon
An he's all alone,
Dere's a man on de moon
His wife is at home.
He's dancing around
To real moony music,
He carries his air
He know how to use it,
He waves to his wife
Still on Planet E,
She's waving back.
But he cannot see.
[...]
Dere's a man on de moon
He has a spaceship,
Dere's a man on de moon
An we payed fe it...

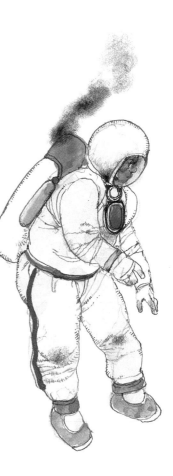

Write, write, write and then rewrite!

When I write my books, I'm a 15-year-old reluctant reader, which is what I was, and I think about what I would have wanted to read. That's where I start.

If I was a young kid now I'd be listening to hip hop music, so why not do a poem on hip hop music? I don't really do much research, especially when it comes to subjects. I just think about what I would have liked to read.

This is the room in my house where I do all my writing.

I write lots of fiction, as well as the poetry, and writing that's different because you have to plan it more. I tend to start at the beginning, and write chapter one, chapter two, chapter three, not always knowing where it's going. Sometimes when I'm stuck, I act it out. I speak it, so I'm capturing the sound. When I'm writing a novel, I can decide to write 6,000 words, and I'll just write, write, write, write. Then afterwards I'll decide what to keep and what to scrap. I've learnt to rewrite as well. I tend to get the immediate thought out and then look at it and think, "Did that work? It sounded good at the time but it doesn't sound so good now."

With poetry I find it really difficult to sit over a blank piece of paper. On the whole I have to give myself some space, a few months when I'm not doing anything, just riding my bike, travelling around, and just let it come. Poetry can't be forced.

I'm not very **disciplined** at sitting down and writing every day, though. If I get up and there are birds singing outside I want to go and listen to them, or go for a run, or if there's a football field I'll go and play football!

What I do now

What I really like about my job is that I do so many different things. I get really excited about things when I start work on them, but after a while I lose excitement, and it's great that I've always got something else to do that's completely different, so I can get excited all over again.

For example, I might be doing a television film of one of my novels, writing a newspaper article or performing internationally, or it could be something totally different – something musical like recording an album. After that I might be happy to sit down and start writing a novel again. It's that variety that I like. I think I was born to do this kind of thing because when I see people going to work and doing the same thing in the same office, I know I couldn't do it. I realise how **privileged** I am, and I really appreciate it.

This is me on the day I was given a degree by the University of Hull, in 2010.

Chilling out

Because I'm still working so hard, I try to find things to do that help me relax. I do a lot of t'ai-chi, which is a form of **kung fu**, and running.

practising t'ai-chi

I've got an old English car which I restore. I used to restore lots of cars but I've only got one now. I also collect money, bank notes from all over the world. It's a serious collection, and some of them are very old and rare.

This is me in the car I restored myself.

And of course I'm an Aston Villa fan. I go to games sometimes – not every Saturday, because I'm not crazy about football, but I was born in Aston and I think you have to be loyal to your local team. I recently started sponsoring a local girls' team and it really got me back into football. They're 11 or 12 years old and watching them made me think about football again, so now I go to the odd Aston Villa match.

From Hong Kong to China

I spend a lot of time in China these days. The first time I went to China was during a trip to Hong Kong. I handed my passport in at the border and went on a day trip to China. I remember coming home and looking at the map and thinking we drove for three hours into China and we only went to the tip of this massive country!

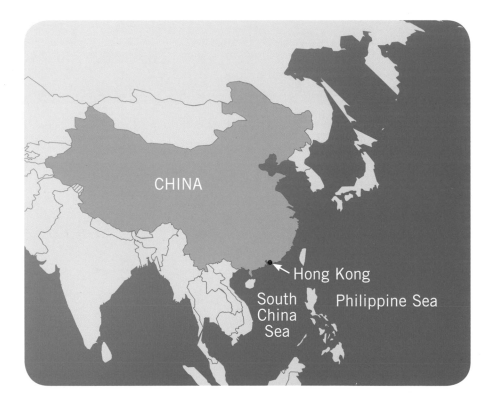

women in China practising t'ai chi

It made me want to see more of the place, and I just fell in love with it. It can be difficult in some ways, and it's a cultural challenge, but it's great for martial arts and I love it there.

I get the same buzz, which I think is really exciting, from travelling as I do from turning up at one of my gigs.

signing books on one of my trips to China

49

A happy feeling

I'm pretty lucky because I don't really have any ambitions left.
I mean I want to do all the things that I'm doing now better,
I love doing them all. I want to write better novels, I want
to write better poetry and I want to write a novel for adults,
but I can't really think of anything else.

This is me making a speech on the day
I was given my West Midlands Minority
Achievement Award in 2009.

I'm at peace with myself and that's what really makes me happy.

Glossary

absurdity   stupidity, ridiculousness

Apartheid   a system in South Africa that forced people of different races to live apart, and gave fewer rights to non-white people

communal   shared by a group of people

disciplined   good at following rules you have set yourself

disassociate   separate

dyslexic   having a condition that makes reading and writing hard. People with dyslexia are often very creative and imaginative

galore   in large numbers

golliwog   a doll with a black face

kung fu   a form of self-defence where people only use their hands and bodies

lifestyle   the way a person lives

minority groups   small groups in society whose views and opinions are not often heard

motivation   the reason for doing something

Nelson Mandela   a man who led many black South Africans in their fight for equal rights and was put in prison for it, but who eventually became South Africa's first black president

opportunities   chances

parables   stories with a message, that show people how to behave

phonetically   based on the sounds of words rather than the way they're spelt

privileged   lucky

Rastafarian   a member of a Jamaican religion that worships the former Emperor of Ethiopia in Africa, Haile Selassie

reluctant   not at all keen

Index

Timeline

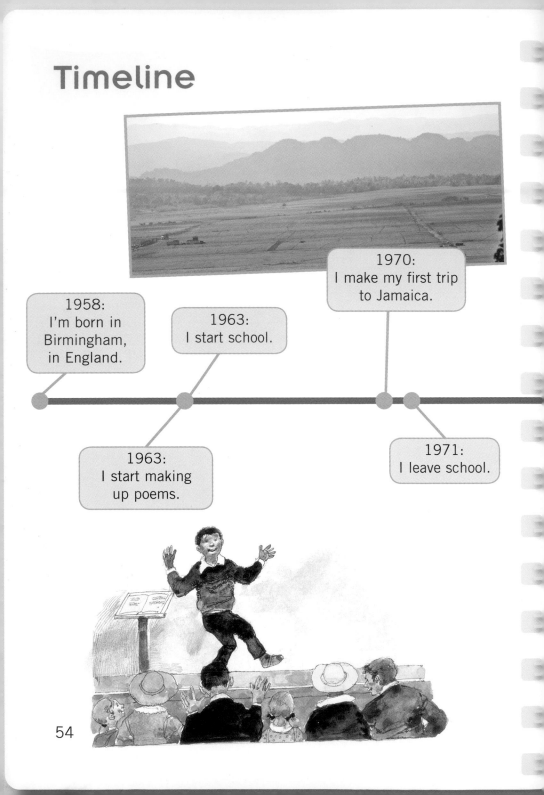

1970:
I make my first trip
to Jamaica.

1958:
I'm born in
Birmingham,
in England.

1963:
I start school.

1963:
I start making
up poems.

1971:
I leave school.

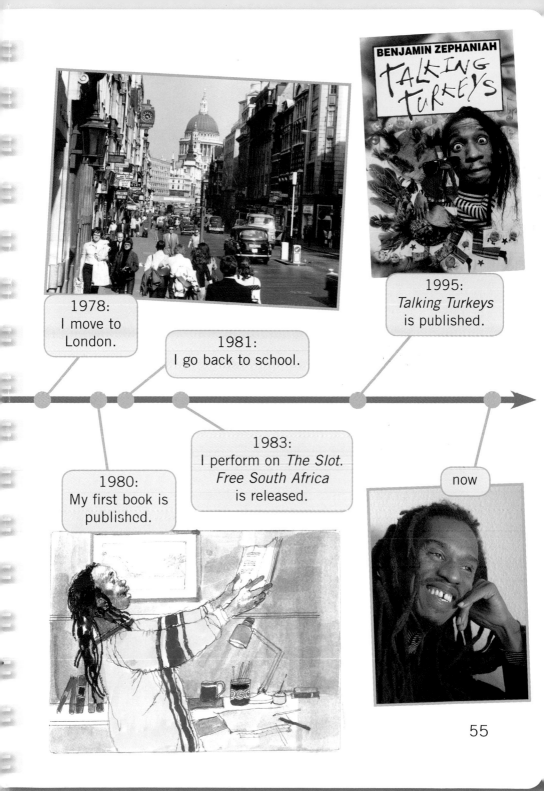

1978:
I move to London.

1981:
I go back to school.

1995:
Talking Turkeys is published.

BENJAMIN ZEPHANIAH
TALKING TURKEYS

1980:
My first book is published.

1983:
I perform on *The Slot*.
Free South Africa is released.

now

55

Ideas for reading

Written by Linda Pagett B.Ed (hons), M.Ed
Lecturer and Educational Consultant

Learning objectives: sustain engagement with longer texts, using different techniques to make text come alive; compare how writers from different places use language; listen for language variation; improvise using a range of drama strategies

Curriculum links: History: How has life in Britain changed since 1948?; Citizenship: Living in a diverse world

Interest words: apartheid, disciplined, disassociate, dyslexic, golliwog, kung fu, minority, mother country, opportunities, parables, phonetically, privileged, Rastafarian, reluctant, t'ai-chi

Resources: writing materials, ICT

Build a context for reading

This book can be read over two or more reading sessions.

- Ask one of the children to read the blurb and then ask the group to discuss other autobiographies they've read. Discuss why people might write an autobiography. Is it simply to tell the story of their life, or might there be another reason?

- Ask children if they have heard any of Benjamin Zephaniah's poems, and if they have, what they think of them. If they haven't, do they have any other favourite poets?

- Turn to the index and glossary and check that the children know how to use them.

Understand and apply reading strategies

- Read the contents together, and discuss the best way to read an autobiography. Can children dip in and out of chapters, or should it be read in order? Why do they think this?

- Ask children to read silently to p21. Discuss what Benjamin's childhood was like and whether they think it was happy, using specific examples from the book to support their points.